November Keepsakes

Poetry & Short Stories

LOLA WILLIS

November Keepsakes
Poetry & Short Stories

Copyright © 2024 by Lola Willis

All rights reserved.

No part of this publication may be reproduced, distributed, or transmitted in any form or by any means, including photocopying, recording, or other electronic or mechanical methods, without the prior written permission of the publisher, except as permitted by U.S. copyright law. For permission requests, contact ailinawillis@gmail.com.

The story, all names, characters, and incidents portrayed in this production are fictitious. No identification with actual persons (living or deceased), places, buildings, and products is intended or should be inferred.

Book Cover by Stasia Burrington
Illustrations by Stasia Burrington

First edition 2024

Print ISBN: 979-8-35097-686-1
eBook ISBN: 979-8-35097-687-8

*For Mark and Cass...
the other two pieces of my heart.*

—*April 2015*

*And for Rain, my precious child.
You leave life and purpose in your passing.
Your mother loves you forever.*

—*August 2024*

Acknowledgments 2024

It's been almost ten years since I wrote my original acknowledgements in April of 2015. Much was different at the time this manuscript was prepared in its original format. The most significant change is that "Forest," our eldest child who transitioned to "Rain" in 2022, passed away in May of this year 2024. She is largely responsible for the publication of this book in that she was one of the greatest advocates for my writing these last few years.

Since the early 2020's, I fell into a period of desolation when writing was more painful and burdensome than it was a relief or a survival tool, so I stopped doing it. On some level, this was painful for my kids, too, as I've always demonstrated passion in pursuit of the creative and taught them to chase their arts with their whole hearts. Surely it was disturbing to see me dormant for so long, especially due to the personal struggles I endured during those years.

But Rain always encouraged me to return to writing. Every time we spoke on the phone, the conversation always seemed to turn to art and creativity and self-care, going hand in hand, and she urged me, "You should write again, Mom."

It took her death to inspire me. So I pulled out this manuscript from 2015, brushed it off and breathed life into it again. *Much has changed.* But the feelings, the purpose of the words, their proper places have not changed. So neither should their acknowledgments.

I give you *November Keepsake's Acknowledgments* 2015.

With greatest love...

Lola Willis

Lola Willis

8.25.2024

Leesville, Louisiana

Acknowledgments 2015

Eighteen years of stepping into the shorebreak and cowering again — that's a long time for someone to believe you can and *will* sail. Mark, you have never doubted me or waxed cynical, and you've never made me feel guilty for running. Thank you, Husband, for sharing a true love with me: one that survives onslaughts and ugliness, and instead becomes breathtaking and unbreakable. I love you, in truth, actively, endlessly. Cass, Soul Sister, thank you from the bottom of my spirit for being always immovably convinced the time would come, and for your prayers of perfect timing. He delivers, always.

Mom — that first journal on my 8th birthday: You put the pen in my hand and gave me permission to use my voice. It's just not possible to sufficiently thank you for that, except for me to give the same to the kids. To Forest, Madison, Sunny, Maile, Sophia, Maxwell, and Penny: You have been the best cheering section and fan base any writer (or mom) could ask for. Now it's your turn to make it happen! Go for it! Brooke, thank you for giving me a sense of excellence and opening my eyes to the brutal but necessary reality of its pursuit. I love you, Sister.

To editor Jenny Meadows of *My Copy Editor*: I am truly honored you chose to share your expertise. Your gift is ever sharpened by your love of the strength and beauty of the written word. My thanks to *The Writer* editor Todd Larson for your thoughtful and gracious investment of your time. Stasia Burrington, you have my most passionate thanks and greatest respect and admiration for your stunning artwork and your otherworldly ability to touch those deepest places in the human heart. Thank you for giving music to the melodies. To Joyce Finn and my dear, dear friends in Writers & Critters critique group: Thank you in every language for your camaraderie and bottomless well of encouragement, for a sense of professionalism, and for helping me find the eye and strength to refine so many of these works. I could never adequately express your value...Group hug!

To my beloved Lafayette, Louisiana: Thank you for sincerely embracing me and caring for me through the darkest seasons. And thank you, Leesville, Louisiana: I am ever indebted to you, for you've been my field of wonder, war, and wisdom; you shape the woman I am. I am home.

All my love...
Lola Willis
4.28.2015
Leesville, Louisiana

Author's Note

Truthful love is never a perfectly assembled and delivered thing. Growth and deepening are at turns euphoric and torturous; I write through it hour by hour, the only healthy way to metabolize feelings larger than I am.

November Keepsakes is a collection of raw moments in a history, some drowning and gasping for breath, some floating, some walking upon the surface, and others emerging altogether. Elation is preserved, pain is cut from me. The words are no longer living but are harmless keepsakes, truth of the woman I've been. I turn them in my hands, relive, then return them to the velvet-lined box until the next is poured and hardened.

Contents

Acknowledgments 2024 i

Acknowledgments 2015 iii

Author's Note v

pain 1

Prologue	3
Mermaid	5
Landfall	6
Debris	9
The Gallery	11
Staged	13
Corruption	15
The Implosion	17
Disposable	19
Come Burning August	21

love 29

'88	31
Seattle Monday	33
Cypress Story	35
Man in Mist	37

Landscape	38
Landmark	40
Forest Fire	42

woman 45

The Trail	47
Marco	50
Nude	52
The 29th Year	54
The Pall	55
Wise	56
The Last Year	57
The Pines of Bonneview Road	59
The Feet of Pele	64

faith 71

Right Morning	73
Still	75
Votive	76
bride	77
Believing Life Leaning	78
Portrait in Linen	80

About the Author 83

About the Artist 85

pain

Prologue

Like waking to learn
the bed you built
with your bare hands
has not been a bed at all,
but a weak wooden sculpture
of splinters and shards.

The house you constructed
around you with
lumber you took
from your own backyard
is not a house at all,
but a balanced arrangement of cards,
stacked end to end,
poised to tumble
with a careless exhale.

And the land that you named
is not your land;
it belongs to something
larger and stronger,
insistent and darker,
and it has no name at all.

So you have only
the skin on your back,
the marks and scars,

(Prologue)

the muscle memory,
the lines beneath in bone
where fissure and fracture
healed over the marrow.

And antibodies flow
in your blood
and will till you're dead,
traces of all the infections
you fought and suppressed.

And now you're immune;
should you fall to the same
affliction again,
you will not succumb.
You will not succumb.
You will not succumb.

Recognize.
I recognize this place
I've visited before.
I'm visited again.
It looks like a beginning,
but feels like an end.

Mermaid

She settled on
the dead seabed
and bent into the
narrow shadows
of all she had,
reading stinging secrets
upon the moon's fifth phase,
bleeding from the
cut of each phrase.
Confessions swam
from her drowned mouth,
and still there was no ease.

Glaciers sheared
of ether and quartz
dropped tainted diamonds
like salt shaken
from the hands
of a sickened sea.
Would-be words
split and scaled,
for the voice was traded
for a land coveted
more than the breath to speak.

Landfall

The stricken blue-wash
of a ravaged winter beach,
naked throat opened
by an angry November storm.
I am gnarled and splintered twists
of primitive wood drunk dry
by a thousand drifts,
and gleaming stubs
of blunt bleached teeth
honed by too many brushes
with sharp colors
far more brilliant than mine.

Swallowing,
bellowing,
mauling mouths
tearing at me again,
and again I am just beyond
the mercy of a higher tide.

A bay of bones,
lame hands
splayed in vain:
Remember days

(Landfall)

alive and thriving,
harbor of seafoam,
harbor of shade,
haven for sand-skinned lovers
or silver women
with sunlit lips and bladed eyes.
The wrists recall,
the fingers recoil
and rest in plain sight,
as if they still bore
a bride's diamond
to set fire to pride.

Palms,
torn and long bled,
beg in humility
cast only by many deaths.
First,
a fine spray from veins
tracing antiquity's hills and caves,
now spilling without shame
through what might have been
the grasp of redemption,
if time had not washed away.

(Landfall)

Lovely,
how bright is a wounded sky
when one trains her eye
high enough to blind
the bare thickets
tangled hard and
weeping at her side.

Debris

I clash.
Like a crushed and faded
cigarette butt thrown
in a state park flowerbed.

The perfect palette
of a newborn October morning;
enduring green St. Augustine
littered with oak's delicate shells;
lofty pine, haughty and higher
than the grandmothers' pew,
stinging the air with
a spray of tart fragrance
like sour wine
or too-old perfume.

I kick a path,
scatter and shatter
the backs of the leaves
at the toes of bright blue boots,
chains clanging at my waist,
protesting the autumn shakes
and dry quiet.

(Debris)

Two things only,
this wood and I share:
cinder-grey skin
and a hard shiver
through every limb.

The Gallery

Dawn shadow slip
from lash to hem,
pour down the hollow halls.

Morning mother,
marble milk,
gloss her empty iris;
cold, pale pearl,
return a touch
to broken cornerstone
and pallor.

Goddess sleeping,
rest requite and rapture;
rest the tumbling breast
and rolling waist;
rest, slow-breath lover.

Still the lips,
hush the high hour;
conjure why the chin is bent,
the pupil fixed,
the ancient ache
perpetuates;
why something in me
cracks and breaks,

(The Gallery)

as if the artist
took my bones and
molded his pain
from my own.

Then dark,
fell the lamps and
climb the veils,
stir and whisper
folded robes.

Resurrect,
sweep wing to wing,
wake haunted souls;
to immortal mortuary,
linger memory's mortal wound;
widows weeping,
faint as feathers,
in their lovers' catacombs.

Staged

I am a stunning estate,
borders trimmed and
flowered in season;
fresh-painted face and
shining pillars;
gleaming, unmarked glass.

But the rooms are sour,
worn, and aged;
tapestries frayed;
brass tarnished;
mahogany rain-stained
and decayed.

The halls cold and widow-still,
rafters rotting from the core,
doorways sinking,
walls sighing under the
weight of their days.

My peace in degrees.
The hour is a glorious thing,
with a roof,
a full belly,
a full house of health.

(Staged)

The day is laborious,
work stalking away
like ungrateful children;
a man so lost,
his own image is gnarled;
a faith under fire and
always at arms.

A winding timeline,
great seam of regret,
haunts and torments,
and even forgiveness
will not quiet it.
Our errors of ways,
though pardoned or waived,
accompany me as a shadow
over even the most glorious hour.

I've done all but sever
self from myself,
still hating the child I was
and the troubled woman
whom I'd become.
Filmy windows witness still,
and even in the most glorious hour,
they dull the brightest shine.

Corruption

It's the same kind of
breaking day,
fall propped on
its rotting trunk,
prey to a hungry gust,
will wind in and
tear the limbs away.

Bloodstone treetop's heresy,
blasphemy on the
plated tongue of a
reclining siren summer.
Oil streams anointing
mud-caked veins,
will freeze harder than terror.

Cicadae skin,
thin and wisping like
a strong vow
bled of conviction
by a lung constricting and collapsing
under the tumble of
a petrified oak.

(Corruption)

A clear lake offers
no reflection,
but only a
dark-deep reservoir,
swallowing up
silt and sadness like
an eye's last light
of recognition.

The Implosion

This star inhaled a
last ragged gasp,
then heaved whistling slivers
into the staring void,
like raindrops racing
from the fade and bleed
of diffusion.
Its desperate, dying
ring of fire
gave a final cry that
drained into the blackness and
folded upon itself as that
frightening, frozen sleep.

In the stillness,
drifting debris and a
marbled mass of
sulfur and brine;
thin fingers slowly
turned to center,
feeling for the eye of the
open vein where the
worst pain is paralysis.

(The Implosion)

One heart,

so dense and

gaping and

gulping,

nothing escapes,

nothing escapes, and

nothing escapes.

The edge of an age

searches the churning galaxy,

yet absent a single sign.

All is lost and

draws away,

forever grieving the end of

safe and sure bearing.

Disposable

You pass me like
flickering black pictures:
distorted.
derailed.
detached. and
flashing on
crumbling crack-plaster
brittle as ash.

In the brighter
slides of time,
I lashed a hand at the
blurring colors to
capture the tail of an
image to keep,
like the smell of
crushed leaves or the
chill of your cold hand
wound around mine or the
glimmering watery light on the
edge of your young blue eye.

Shaky frames
fell away for a
series of bleeding moments
overexposed:

(Disposable)

flawed.

lost.

sun-faded.

dust-laden.

forgotten as soon as the

album was closed.

Come Burning August

We were always a pair, Clara an' me — ever since we were small. Mama kept expectin' us to leave, and when we didn't, she left instead — took off with a foreman from Houston. Even when we were grown and I got married, my sister was still with me. She helped with the wedding, keepin' the house up, and then later on, keepin' my husband Charles fed and in clean work clothes. I nursed her through a bout of scarlet fever, a hellcat love triangle, and a broken engagement.

We were sisters, all right. Loved each other better than Mama ever did. And Charles loved us like the daddy we never had. We were a fine family, the three of us. Never needed nothin' else.

We had our moments, though. Clara was a willful one. I had to put my foot down many a time. And if my foot weren't heavy enough, Charles stepped in.

When me and Charles'd have it out, Clara'd be right by me, dressin' him down. Or dressin' me down, whichever served her best at the time.

They were just tiffs. Came and went like the scorching summers. Was cooler times, mostly. Happy times. Better times than they ever were when Mama was home. With Charles, we were a bona fide family. I thought we'd be together till we was all dead. And after that, we'd still be together, six-foot-under and half-a-foot-apart in Roe Methodist Cemetery. I never considered things'd be no different. Never reckoned she'd leave.

One Christmas, she told the both of us she got a job in Biloxi, and come next Sunday, she was gone. The house might

(Come Burning August)

as well've been empty, 'cause it sure didn't feel like no one lived there no more.

    It was bad for a long time. I just sat in the parlor curled up like I was dyin'. Charles kept workin' up at the mill, and he took up my chores around the house, too. God bless 'im, he tried. I never spoke a word to 'im, but he talked to me anyways. He held me a lot and told me how happy Clara probably was, gettin' out of Roe and on her own. She was probably the happiest she ever been.

    Took me a long time to settle with it, but by spring, the house was steady again. It was nice, just me and Charles. At first, I didn't much like all the time with him. I missed our family. Felt like someone done cut an arm from the both of us. But after awhile, it was nice, bein' able to sit quiet together, or lay into each other in the middle of the afternoon, if we're so inclined. We never had a honeymoon. Never went no place special together. But now, it was just the two of us. Never been like that before, and I like to think we both enjoyed it.

    Summer came 'round, and we still didn't hear from Clara. I thought her job must be goin' real well, and I didn't blame her for not sendin' word. I hoped she was happy. I hoped she made somethin' of herself. I hoped she never had to come back to Roe.

(Come Burning August)

I was standin' on the porch in August. The sun was blisterin'. Charles was bent under the house, hoein' up snake nests, when a taxi-cab pulled up in the yard. Out stepped my sister, with three sacks and a baby in her arms.

I ran hollerin' right past my husband, "Clara! Clara!" I hugged her tight, tryin' to cry over her shoulder so she wouldn't see how much I missed her. I swear, I held on for dear life...Clara, them three sacks of hers, and that little babe all mashed between us.

She finally broke loose of me. I looked around for Charles. I wanted him to share the moment, but he already done walked off somewhere.

Inside the house, I sat Clara down and made her some iced tea. She smiled at that baby as she nursed him. I was content to sit with her in the kitchen, and we spent most of the afternoon that way.

Supper was quiet. I wondered what kind of trouble she got herself into that she'd show up at the front door with a baby. I knew Clara, and I'd just let her tell me in her own good time.

Charles didn't say a word. I thought he might be mad she didn't call ahead of time and let us know she was comin'. There were layoffs at the mill; he might be wrung a little tight, havin' two extra mouths to feed.

But he never said one way or the other. He went to bed early. Just as well, 'cause I got a chance to sit with my sister and talk a little before the baby woke up again. She didn't say much, but she seemed happy. I was happy for her.

(Come Burning August)

Next mornin' was the same. Clara spent most of the day in her old bedroom with her little one. She came out every now and then to get a bite to eat. The house felt right, havin' her home again. It was nice just knowin' she was there, that I could go up the stairs and down the hall and see her sittin' there. The evenin' came in slow and silent. Charles tinkered with the stove while I peeled potatoes, and Clara leaned on the fridge sippin' tea and chompin' on a cabbage heart.

Charles got two burners to workin', but when one fizzled out, he said I'd have to make do with the one for now. Then he took off to the property line to mend a length of fence that come unstrung. I watched him from the kitchen window while I chopped onions for the cabbage.

The sun was goin' down. Clara went outside and wandered to where Charles was. They talked for while, looked like. Lord knows they had plenty catchin' up to do. Tears made it hard to see. They were good onions. I wiped my eyes with the back of my hand and split open another one.

They talked on for a while, then Clara changed. She started wavin' her hands, pointin' at the house and grabbin' at Charles's shirtsleeve. My husband was shakin' his head and walkin' away, but she followed him, wavin' her hands more, defiant-like, just like she been ever since we shared the same bed. I knew by the way she held her head high, and by the way Charles looked at the ground, they were arguin'.

(Come Burning August)

Tears were spillin' onto the cutting board. The onion was stronger than the last. I held on tight to the dern thing. I couldn't get a hold of it, and it kept slippin' out of my hands. Thought for sure I was gonna cut myself. I wiped my face with my shoulder and looked out across the yard.

Charles got a distance from Clara, turned around, and hollered somethin' else, pokin' his finger at her. Then he threw his hat on the ground and stomped off toward the shed. Clara screamed so loud, I was certain Pastor Wilson heard her all the way 'cross the other side of the cotton field.

Clara caught herself and yanked her head toward the kitchen. It was far, but we saw each other.

The baby started cryin' then, and I felt sick to my stomach all of a sudden. My thumb stung, and I knew I cut myself. The baby was yellin', I was cryin' and bleedin', but I didn't take my eyes off Clara. She didn't quit lookin' at me neither. Not for a long while. Her, down by the fence, and me, cryin' and bleedin' all over the onions at the kitchen sink.

I sat at the supper table, legs danglin' over my chair. Mama's white lace tabletop barely reached my chin. She stood at the stove, leanin' over her big cast iron pot, stirrin' somethin' with a long wooden spoon. The smell of somethin' awful came bubblin' up from the pot, fillin' the air in the kitchen with the hot, thick stink of rotted meat. Smelled so bad, I thought I'd choke to death.

(Come Burning August)

Mama didn't pay no mind. She wiped the sweat off her face with an old rag hangin' from her apron and stirred and stirred.

"Mama? Is our supper burnin'?" I asked.

"No, lamb. 'Sposed to smell like that," she said.

The smell got worse, and I covered my mouth and nose with my napkin. "Mama, I don't wanna eat that!" I whined.

"Well, that's all we got to eat!" she snapped. Her face wrinkled up, all red and angry. "You got to eat it! You hear me, girl? You GOT TO!"

I woke up gaggin'. I blinked my eyes and saw nothin' but dark. Couldn't tell if it was real or a dream.

I felt next to me for my sister. I grabbed hold of her shoulder and shook her, but it wasn't Clara at all. Charles grunted in his sleep. I was grateful. Way back when Mama was with us, she never yelled at us much, but when she did, even in a dream, it left me shakin' and feelin' sorry.

I strained my eyes to see. The smell didn't go away. It was real. It was strong.

I climbed out of bed, leavin' Charles snorin' alone, and stepped down the hall, floorboards creakin' under my feet. The smell was real bad, but it didn't seem as heavy by Clara's room. I peeked in. She and the baby were still sleepin'.

Back toward our bedroom, the smell got stronger and stronger. Smelt like it was comin' from downstairs.

Halfway to the kitchen, the air just about knocked me out. I covered my mouth and nose with my nightgown, smotherin'

(Come Burning August)

back my coughs. I come up to the kitchen door, and then I knew what it was. Gas from the broken stove flowed freely.

A second later, the kitchen blew to pieces. The door burst apart, kickin' me back against the wall, headfirst. Next thing I knew, fire was eatin' up the walls all around me. I couldn't see the ceiling for all the smoke.

I jumped to my feet and ran for the stairs, hollerin' for Charles and Clara at the top of my lungs. My face felt sunburnt. My nightgown soaked with sweat and stuck to my skin. It hurt to breathe. The back of my head throbbed where it hit the wall, and I was still a little dizzy, but I kept yellin', all the way back to the stairs.

By the time I turned up the steps, the banister already caught. Flames filled the first floor, up to the foyer. I didn't know how we'd make it out before the fire took it all.

Clara crouched at the top of the stairs, screamin'. Charles come up behind her and grabbed her back from the fire, but my sister flailed her arms at him and disappeared back down the hall. I started up toward my husband, but the flames took the top steps.

Charles shouted at me to get outside, but I didn't move. Then here come Clara, still screamin'. She had an armful of blankets, and I told her to beat back the fire with them. She didn't pay me no mind. Her eyes rolled around in their sockets; she was yellin' my name.

(*Come Burning August*)

Charles ran into the bathroom and came back with the trashcan full of water. He dumped it into the fire, but it didn't do no good. The flames grew higher. They licked up the walls and spread across the ceiling. I couldn't see through them no more.

Clara let out an awful shriek, and a bundle of blankets shot at me through the fire. I caught them. They were heavy, and they started to move. The baby's muffled cries reached my ears, and I panicked. I backed off the stairs and watched as the fire ate up the last part of the hallway I could see.

I ran outside, away from the fire and away from Clara's screamin'. I ran down the gravel road and past the gates, far-far from the house, but I could still hear Clara screamin'. Then, her screamin' became their screamin', and I ran. I ran and I ran, into the dark, as far away from the house as I could get. I kept runnin', and I never looked back.

The night was black as pitch. The baby was gettin' heavy, and I stumbled along, switchin' it from arm to arm. It was probably asleep by then, 'cause it hadn't made a sound for a long time. I still couldn't see a thing, just kept movin' on through the dark.

I knew where I was, though. Felt the road under my bare feet. I just kept walkin'. I didn't stop. I knew if I kept goin', I'd make it to town no matter what.

love

'88

She recalled
what it was like
in the dark,
in the minutes that
stretched like an hour,
her belly a swarm of
flitting things and the
way her breath
dragged in and she
could already taste him
on the air.

She remembered
the ripe silence and
how she tried to
fill it with words
that mattered, and
how courage reared and
retreated time after time,
her eyes always on the
line of his lips.

She remembered
his fine hair
in her fingertips when the
stadium lights burned out, and

('88)

urgency leapt, and
the last pair of taillights
turned out of sight.

So prolonged,
and when the kiss met,
it billowed and heaved
like a thunderhead
climbing the sky.

His hair was
no longer fine,
his hands
no longer soft and unmarked,
but his lips were as
engulfing as they'd been
fifteen years before,
and now,
when the lights went down,
there was all the
time in the world, and
she let it storm
till there was
no rain left to fall.

Seattle Monday

Like trying to capture the
exactness of a single color
from the window of
a passing train.
The only muscle of
perception and memory
I have is the repressed,
and the aftertaste
on my tongue
brings to mind
the softness and warmth of a
clean cow's hide on a
Seattle Monday.

I am guessing
he is the equivalent of a
dying tree
too-long trapped in a
pit of dirt on a
crosswalk corner.
(And the funny thing is,
under all that
steel and concrete is the
cool, wet soil, to which –
given enough time –
all would return,

(Seattle Monday)

the divine primary palette restored,
and his God could rest in the
slack of a once-strained spectrum.
I am guessing he'd
prefer to be buried.)

If this train
slowed or stopped,
I would be the only one

to notice the contrast of the
bright, rich shreds of
tobacco scattered on the
thick-mixed asphalt,
and there have been times
when I've glimpsed
my fingers
on his skin and
thought the same.

Coffee stains and
dried blood,
and the edge of his coat,
all look the same
from this passing window.

Cypress Story

Hide me in your hand,
in something more beautiful,
where you are the beautiful one,
and I adrift,
with fewer words
than your muted green and
sundrops sliding down
a waxy bough.

What am I that
I do not understand
your ancient language
written in the tall and narrow script
of the cypress knees,
or the silver-flashing syllables
of diamondback eddies,
or even the long, low song
of the brush,
enfolding me in timber arms and
damp shoulder-moss?

Like a love letter,
that blade cuts silent and
smooth through warm glass,
like I am as natural as the
speckled moccasin
essing like a heartbreak

(Cypress Story)

that won't be helped.
Press me to your palm,
close your knotted fingers
one by one,
and grow up thick over
where I entered in,
and I shall never again
think on anything
but the smell of the

lingering season and
how the bend turns
ever to a peaceful end
the very same as this one.

Man in Mist

A feeling immortal,
pulsing through our years,
as tide and mist,
as earthquake,
as breath,
as kiss.

You are rain,
you are ice,
you are grey suede
and bone-salt.
You flood,
you retreat,
you leave ache bare
and bleached
and burned.

Taut spine and
unbending limb,
cooled touch,
splintered skin.
I have always
wrapped tight to
your crooked frame,
will always thread
through the arches of
your crowns and shadows same.

Landscape

On the slopes of meridian,
cast down from the
closing corners of the
folding evening hour,
a storm came like a whisper,
and with it brought the
faint tastes of November
(that November,
brushing grey suede
along the edges of the
edges of youth
tamed and bridled in
fettered promise;
that November that
swept aside brazen color and
dusted ash and
cold timber like
a century rain),
clinging,
tressed and splendid,
to vacant hills and thriving
among the bowing
reeds of spring.
The smoke lingered,
stole one's breath,
and settled deep
under the frozen soil.

(Landscape)

The haunting song of that
winter spear
came all too soon,
carried a sleeping season
aloft,
drove ever west,
catching at the
unraveling hem of a
fleeing fog.

Landmark

This hazing decade
has rounded under your hands,
finely ribboned,
rich and tanned.
You remain
the grandest structure,
this era's monument.

I was steel and granite,
and iron and glass,
a twisting bridge
suspended
by tension and wire,
arches sweeping
the sharp skyline.
Your gusts
howled and thrashed
against each bolt,
resistance and give.
How loud the cables sang
and did not snap.

Now,
I am soil,
cool and damp,
trembling grain by grain
under the shallowest turns.

(Landmark)

I lie,
erode,
and dissolve.
But always
beneath you.

Forest Fire

Air stream
burned clean,
a raw cold
breath sting.
Salt on the eyes
washed in fog,
clings to soaked skin
and stringy hair.
Heat sealed
in denim,
and the smell
of a forest fire.

And torn,
limp leaves and
grainy soil on
sneaker soles.
Your mouth was a
steaming drink and the
shock of your
block-chilled hands on the
crack of my spine,
and the cloud of smoke and
blindness from your throat.

(Forest Fire)

Lost on the trails
back there,
the dead grey of
dead wood like char
where a fire
licked and died.
Pine needle fragrance
distilled in the musk
of red river clay.

woman

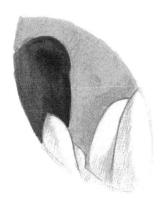

The Trail

7:10 AM,
a backpack slung,
stuffed with scuffed and
faded texts.
I should've been
well read,
prepared for the
brutal adult world ahead.
Cultured,
educated,
networked,
applied.

My neighborhood street,
damp like a
night spent crying,
the gravel traveling
fast beneath my feet.
I raced like a heartbeat
to the trees.

The path,
sparse grass,
sloped back into haze,
snaked around bends,
over rotting moss-laden logs,

(The Trail)

across a murky and
struggling creek
fit for no life but
crushed Coke cans and
Michelob piss.

Every morning,
muster call,
but oh! how I delayed

in the haze with the
wood-chipping,
the chirping,
the hissing,
the caws.
And the rotting moss-laden logs and the
dripping fingers of the creek, and the
fresh smoke from my lungs,
color the same as the reservoir fog.

The forest held me
in its breath,
rejecting I was less
and never enough,

(The Trail)

spared the cold red brick
and ammonia-shined halls,
the warped clanging of lockers,
the sharp-slamming trapdoor.

More than once
I almost dropped it all,
almost escaped
into the haze to
broader rotting moss-laden logs,
deeper creeks,
thicker fog.
Beyond,
I might emerge
in a place
far removed
where I could sleep,
in a house of fallen leaves.

Marco

The bottle rolled
from her fingertips
into the sea,
turned into
envy-green folds of
glass and foam,
drew farther and farther
from the shore
like a wakened son
from his mother's warm side.

The sand for her feet,
the sun for her cheeks,
and the wind —
to encircle,
envelope,
to hold,
to keep
all her parts sewn up
like the seams of
a paper sail
that would not see the
greater latitude lines.

One possession she owned,
cut from her heart,

(Marco)

from her hand,
from the hem of her
thin linen gown and
wrapped up in a scroll.

A prayer
that the words
would not drown,
but survive

at the breast of the
heaving green sea,
carried abroad
with a name and the
hour seized
at the moment the
ink stained the page.

And she counted the
days in waiting,
in faith,
for the answering cry
to return on the crown
of a white noonday tide.

Nude

Smooth tumble and roll
under warm rays,
slumber in high noon,
laid thin and
heavy pressed on the
cool brown ground.
Arid song spilling
from a tired throat,
of a day fully spent,
body unfolded and
so pouring untouched.

A drop of dream,
sparkling on the
end of a frond,
resting,
relieved,
a black needle sleeping.

From the
breast of the desert,
wind shifting
like a snaking sigh,
sweeping skirts across the
rippling horizon.

(Nude)

Whistling bones bury a
once-mighty river,
drained to the
last thirsty cloud.

Canyon yawning
another year as a
first-drawn breath,
thoughtless drifts
turn trudging toward dusk,

or still,
a nomad alone
tracing time
through unmarked sky and
barebacked land.
Waking,
a thorn pricking the
center of the palm
on one hand.

The 29th Year

Comb fine black wax
that poured like oil
in newer days,
down a back
softer and unbroken.
Steps were young,
and they were sure,
long and wide in stride.
Just,
the shores of beauty shift,
leave slivers of
auburn and dusty rose,
edges softer and unbroken.
The year's marks:
strokes in curves,
some deep,
some shallow,
all distinct
upon the dunes.
Yet the landscape,
softer and unbroken.

The Pall

The years' used
And the wear of other coats
Give way to pull out
The sealed trunks.
Try on the old clothes,
And recall the black feathers
Of those sharp, shining crows
And their pricking clips—
Plucked now and thinned down
To bare bird bones.
They flap from the moth balls,
Pecking my head
To see what worms still curl
In pockets and pages,
Black and white wiggling
For a bite.

Wise

The shore was awash
at dusk that day with
crumbling fragments
of chalky decay,
inlaid in the
glossy satin sand
like petrified spines.
I encircled them,
arcing wide,
tracks melted by the
receding tide.

Returning debris on the
lip of the sea,
an impulse stayed:
I've seen the
hearts when whole,
before the battering elements
broke upon them,
dashing to cloud
precious coral and ivory bowls.

I turned and withdrew,
for good this time,
sea oats hip-high,
bare feet dry.

The Last Year

Pull the late year
around my shoulders
like moonlit silk,
slim fingers as curled as
dried grapevines.

Life woven behind,
heavy with
imperfect design and the
fragrance of lavender dust and
rose petals pressed.

A milk jar at my heel,
filled with vinegar
clear and distilled.
And strung at my side,
burnt ivory keys
lined in a row of
measured refrain,
pulse muted and strained.

My parlor windows wide,
curtains parted,
rustling like the hush of a
comforted widow's sighs.

(The Last Year)

The last year
will be a
veil of spun web,
glistening,
brief as a
departing whisper or
a dim flicker
across the cloudy surface of a
marbled grey eye.

The Pines of Bonneview Road

The woods swallowed Kimberly Paul.

Roe High School, '89. Our senior year. There were seven of us on Bonneview Road. We dressed in chains and black T-shirts, and thought the bus was for pussies. Each morning we cut through the forest that barreled in from the edge of the parish to the campus grounds. The pines were black and thick, stabbing up from the wet earth and piercing the soft belly of the December sky. We tore through groping spider webs, trampled fallen pine needles, kicked through the oily creek to reach the high school campus.

The woods guarded our skeletons. We skipped class back there and smoked cigarettes just inside the tree line. We lurked in the off-shoot paths with cases of warm beer, shaking our fists and banging our heads to the thrash and rumble of Iron Maiden. When our blood got hot, we ran like fever, deep into the brush where the paths ended, where we could no longer hear the coaches screaming on the field, and they couldn't hear us grunting and hissing like bobcats.

The city of Roe didn't own the property at all — it belonged to us, the Bonneview kids; we claimed every square mile of its glorious rot and dampness.

And then the woods took Kimberly Paul.

It began as a whisper of smoke pulling from Roger Mitchell's lips. He was the red-haired football player who always had the weed and the word. He told us she was missing.

(The Pines of Bonneview Road)

Kimberly Paul was one of the good kids, a bus-rider. She lived at the end of the street and kept her distance. She was curvy, heart-shaped pink face, pretty. And she had great hair — long and bleached blonde, with a perfect spiral perm everyone else tried to duplicate. She was in Honor class and on Student Council, and she never skipped school, but Roger said she did Thursday morning, and she never made it home that night. That's why, he said, all the cops were at Principal Murphy's office first thing Friday and why the woods were now declared off-limits.

The new rule didn't stop us. Teachers blocked the main path into the woods, so we just took another. We loitered in a circle at the edge of the creek, passing around Marlboros, flicking butts into the pitchy brown water, and swapping theories — she ran off with a soldier from Fort Wesley, she got knocked up and was probably staying with her grandma in Florien, or it was all a lie some asshole started to give RHS something to talk about over Christmas break.

The winter wind scraped at our faces. The naked pines pointed up like iron stakes into the sweeping, ashy sky — not a shudder in the afternoon chill. We pulled our coats tight around us and stared into the shadows, expecting to see a flash of denim or a streak of complexion. But the woods were still, like a blurry old photograph. We listened for a call or a cry from deep in the forest, but the only sounds came from the gurgling creek and the clinking chains on our boots and jackets.

(The Pines of Bonneview Road)

Weeks passed. One by one, we abandoned the path and walked the cold, straight route down Bonneview Road. The pavement skirted the woods, but we kept to the opposite side of the street, averting our eyes from the thick wall of trees and the darkening shade of black on the drying bark.

Eventually, vines and poison ivy strangled the path entrance. None of us stepped foot into the forest, but we all remembered the wet, burned smell of dead leaves, and the film of dank air on our skin. By spring break, most of us took the bus, including Roger Mitchell.

One day near the end of the school year, Roger caught up with us at the bus line. He offered to share a joint with us behind the gym, but we passed. Then he said he found something back in the woods.

We followed him to the path. The ground was clear of our litter, our crushed cigarette butts and beer bottles buried in mud puddles and mangled overgrowth.

Roger led us in about twenty paces, then cut a sharp right off the trail. About a stone's throw, tucked in a mat of briar, was a pink canvas bag, caked with dirt and stained from rain.

It could be anyone's bag, stolen, rummaged, and tossed into the trees. Nothing anyone would want — textbooks, a hairbrush, a cracked case of makeup. But when we pried open a water-logged Science book, there, scratched in pink, bubbly letters, was her name — *Kimberly Paul*.

(The Pines of Bonneview Road)

We backed away from the book, wiping our hands on our jeans. Roger spat on the ground; someone cursed. We edged toward the trail, scanning the ground for a sign from Kimberly Paul, listening for her voice. Only the violent, rushing wail of blood gorging our veins and leaves crunching under our shoes.

We took off back toward the school, out of the decaying woods, leaving the books, the brush, the makeup, and whatever else remained. Roger left campus, but the rest of us tracked down Principal Murphy and told him what we saw. He told us to show him where the bag was, but without Roger, we wouldn't go back. We told him where to find it.

We expected the cops to come back with their dogs and their yellow tape. We expected a morning announcement, at least. Instead, the school had a pep rally. There was no talk of Kimberly Paul again. We graduated and moved away.

A couple of years later, the school board bought five acres of woods. They carved into the hip of the forest and tore our trees to the ground. They built a new track and a stadium, paved over the path and the creek, and buried every secret and deed under concrete bleachers.

Every time we went home for the holidays, we scanned the Missing posters on the QuickMart bulletin board. Kimberly's yearbook picture was still stapled in the same dusty corner. Date of birth, date missing, last seen on Roe High School campus. There was no mention of the woods.

(The Pines of Bonneview Road)

Last year, they executed a man in Huntsville. He took a little girl from the fair and murdered her in the woods near the state line. Down at the Country Skillet, Miss Mavis heard some of the city cops say the man lived in Roe the year Kimberly disappeared, that he called in sick to his job on the day she went missing. He never confessed to it, but the Sheriff's Office locked away the file, convinced it was him.

We went home for the ten-year reunion this last October. We sat in the new bleachers with our kids, waving pennants and hollering at the coaches.

But behind the thundering bandstand, just beyond the reach of the stadium lights, the school board's expanded property line stopped dead at the forest wall. The jagged silhouette of the treetops bled into the blueblack sky.

If we were still seventeen, we would've left the game to wander back into the dark, to share a smoke or a kiss or a bottle of JD. The kids of Bonneview Road were back there now, hiding in their woods, content with a light jacket to keep out the chill.

The Feet of Pele

My sister was still with us that spring in Hilo. Uncle Joe said Rosie and I were finally ready to join our hula sisters on the stage of the great festival. Soon, the best *hālaus* from every island would gather to dance before our elders. We danced to honor our late King Kalākaua, the Merrie Monarch, whose love for our people saved our hula from the burial of time.

For three days, Rosie and I had not been home, or to work, or to classes. We stayed with the hālau, and with Uncle Joe. The first day, we followed our aged, limping *kumu* into the upland forests of Hoʻokena to harvest maile for our wrists and ankles. The next day, to Puʻu Makaʻala, to gather red and yellow lehua for our leis.

That night, we followed Uncle Joe down to the shore, for *kapu kai*. We bathed in the black tide. The salt water folded over our heads and carried our sins far out to sea. Now, Uncle Joe said, we were ready for our final rite — our visit to Pele.

The last morning, Uncle Joe led us to Halemaʻumaʻu, to the cold, yawning bed where Pele slept. We climbed the barren path, our feet chilled and bloody on the jagged lava rock.

We stood at Pele's sharp collarbone, peering deep into her ashy throat. We huddled together for warmth while tongues of smoking sulfur lifted from the dry, cracked earth. Uncle Joe chanted and prayed. He leaned his bent body into the raking wind, calling and calling to Pele.

One by one, we came forward to offer our *hoʻokupu*. We turned our stinging skins to Pele's face and hurled our gifts

(The Feet of Pele)

far out into her belly — leis of flowers and seeds, branches of fruiting ʻōhelo berries, bundles of other valuables tied up in ti leaves. In return, she would give her blessing. The festival would come, we would dance before our gathered generations, and we would be perfect.

Pele did give her blessing. Our hula was perfect. But our *mana* did not match that of the Kuakahi family of Molokaʻi. Their feet carried a greater blessing of Pele's power.

Uncle Joe took his lei to the elder Kuakahi. They embraced, eyes proud and serious, and then we all went home.

Rosie left the hālau that summer. She fell in love with an Army chaplain, Dan. At her wedding, Uncle Joe limped down the aisle, his chant shivering from his old throat like moths. The soldiers watched him pass, their lips twisted like wire.

Rosie wore a veil, the kind that dragged the ground behind her. Many chose veils, because *lei poʻo* looked strange on the bride of a man in uniform.

The day they left for Fort Worth, Uncle Joe would not come out. Rosie brought a lei she made from Mother's pīkake. She left her shoes at the door and disappeared inside. My sister came out crying. Her hands covered her face, and a ti leaf was tied around her wrist. She left with Uncle Joe's blessing and protection.

(The Feet of Pele)

At the airport, Rosie kissed me and slipped a lei over my head. Seven strands of gleaming wiliwili seeds, woven into a thick shining rope of red. It was the last lei Rosie ever made.

After Dan's discharge, the church sent them to the mission in Guatemala. The streams rotted my sister's insides. She curled up in the back of the chapel and slipped away, two years after Janet was born.

The next year, we danced in mourning. Hālau was not the same without Rosie. Uncle Joe pushed us fiercely. He did not rest in the week before the festival. He sat in his chair, leaning on the bruised crook of his cane, growling at us and shaking his finger. "'*Ai ha'a!* Lower!" he said. "Steady shoulders! *Hana hou!* Again! Again!"

We danced through breakfast, through lunch. We polished the floor with our sweat and tears we were forbidden to cry. Virgie collapsed from the heat, and Uncle Joe put her in the back. Le'a couldn't hold it anymore, and when she ran to the *lua*, Uncle Joe would not let her back in.

We danced until we were almost perfect. But we would not be perfect until we saw Pele.

Pele would be pleased with my ho'okupu. Rosie's lei, carefully wrapped in ti leaves, vanished over the crater's edge.

Uncle Joe refused to stand for the cameras. The other kumus spoke for him, praising his tradition.

We saw ourselves on the news. "*Auē!* There's Le'a! There's Malia!"

(*The Feet of Pele*)

The newspapers said we were the finest hālau to take the stage. "Hawaiʻi's own." Better, even, than the Kuakahi family of Molokaʻi.

Uncle Joe grunted at our photo and said he was finished. He gave the hālau to his niece and went home.

A young woman called from the mainland. Her voice was like Rosie's, but Rosie never said "ya'll."

"Our hālau's comin' to Hilo, Aunty," Janet said. I didn't know there were hālaus in Texas.

"You going dance, Kuʻulei?" I asked.

"Yes, ma'am."

"You going see Pele?"

"Well, no, Aunty, I can't do that." She called to her father.

Dan cleared his throat into the phone. He talked about Rosie being a good Christian. He talked about God's jealousy. I thought we were all good Christians, and I didn't know there could be anyone more jealous than Pele.

Janet's kumu was not like Uncle Joe. Shiny boots poked out from under his slacks, and there was no grey on his head. A kumu's *kīhei* wouldn't suit him. But on the festival stage, with maile draped down his body, he was not a *hapa haole* teacher from the mainland, but a strong, proud young kumu hula. His chant was old, like his lineage. I knew his mother; she came from the same line as Uncle Joe.

(The Feet of Pele)

The drums began, and Janet danced. She moved like Rosie; her hula was almost perfect.

But on the last verse, the line was broken. Janet's foot slipped, her knee collapsed under her thick *kapa* skirts.

In the audience, something snapped, as if a giant hand reached in and broke our spines. The people turned toward the thrones; the court sat looking down at their hands.

My niece rose from the floor, shivering and stone-faced. The *pahu* drums thundered louder, ordering her feet — "re-*turn*, re-*turn*...." Janet lifted her chin and returned.

But the chant was lost. Soon, the drums stopped. The mana of their hula bled away into the wood floor. Janet and her hula sisters left a silent stage.

I did not go to see her in the dressing room. At the hotel, Janet came to the door, flushed and sick. She buried her face in my lei. "I'm so sorry, Aunty!"

"Shh, Kuʻulei.... *Mai uē,* dry your tears, now."

"Kumu asked me why, Aunty, I don't know what happened."

"Shh...nevamine you, *ke keiki.*" I thought of Halemaʻumaʻu. I thought of Rosie's lei resting across Pele's breasts. I should have gone to Pele myself.

"Come, Kuʻulei. Your aunties are waiting at the ʻahaʻaina. Come eat, kay?"

(The Feet of Pele)

The hanging lamps burned blue against the tarp the cousins raised in the yard. Uncle Richard and his brothers sat near the cooler, thumbing their ukuleles and sending harmonies into the fragrant wet night. Flies circled the laulau and poi. The aunties fanned them away with their hats.

"Your niece going dance, yah?" Cousin Lorraine sat next to me and put a plastic cup of beer in my hands. "She going dance now, Aunty."

Uncle Richard coughed and stood. He raised his hand until it was quiet. "Aunty," he said, "Janet going dance for you. An' for your sister, Aunty Rosie, God-rest-her-soul."

He turned to his brothers. "*E Ku'u Lei....*"

Janet stepped into the grass. A lei made from Mother's pīkake hung from her neck. She wore the dress I made for Rosie when we were still in high school, white with printed garlands of maile and ginger threading down the fabric. Uncle Richard began to sing, and Janet raised her hands to tell a story of longing, of a lover's return.

My sister's daughter was perfect. Her small feet met the earth and melded into the soil like rainwater. The trade winds blew in from the bay and filtered through her hands, catching at her hair and the fringed palm high above. The waters of Waipi'o flowed downstream from her fingers and emptied at the corners of my eyes.

Rosie sighed inside me, returning home from her travels, like tiny seeds drifting on the currents of the sea.

(The Feet of Pele)

What kind of hula was this? Old and familiar, but born of something else.

Pele was far away, sleeping deep beneath the ashes at Halemaʻumaʻu. She did not care that Janet danced for me and my dead sister, or that we gave no hoʻokupu, for my niece was perfect. Better than Rosie and I, better even than the Kuakahis of Molokaʻi. I did not know where this hula came from, this blessing that was not Pele's.

faith

Portrait in Linen

The firm and conscious snap
of a smooth drape of linen,
unscrolling from the bolt
like holy words
penned and black on the
aged pages of a hymnal,
an old spiritual
rolls in the throat,
black eyes cast low
along trim folds,
glistening pins,
steel and sharp like the
sting of fire in the soul.

The soles of
soft worn shoes
brush below
slate grey skirts,
whispering along the floor
like the hush of wings,
and the peek of dry hands,
arched and aching and
soothed on the grain,
piecing together
straight temple curtains,
sound and seamlessly
as years fitted at tender hems.

(Portrait in Linen)

A shroud fashioned
of patient silence,
natural light,
and a portrait of artistry
etched in the heart
like a grandmother's maiden name.

About the Artist

Stasia Burrington is a Japanese-American artist living and working in Seatac, WA, with her favorite people and two cats. She is a kind and curious illustrator and storyteller, with over 30 years of image-and-object making experience.

She has illustrated a best-selling children's Book (*Mae Among the Stars*, by Roda Ahmed), and is the creator of the well-loved Sasuraibito Tarot deck. She has been honored with the "Master of Erotic Art" title by the Foundation for Sex Positive Culture in 2020.

She now creates and ships tarot decks and artwork all over the world.

She is a full-time artist/illustrator. She is into mycology, foraging, music, camping, fat nerdy science books, coffee, noodles, and ice cream.